DOUBLE YOUR
WEBSITE TRAFFIC

DOUBLE YOUR WEBSITE TRAFFIC

A STEP-BY-STEP BLUEPRINT USING CONTENT, SEO, PPC, AND SOCIAL MEDIA

RYAN MORGAN

ISBN: 9781695239920

www.theDoubleBook.com

CONTENTS

Introduction **9**

Content Marketing **13**

Content Audit 14

  Keep, Update, Combine, Delete.........................14

Content Strategy 18

  Choose Your Topics 18

  Topic Selection: Choosing the Right Topics by Focusing on High Volume, Low Competition Keywords 22

  Plan and Write Your Content (or Outsource It!)........25

How to Write High-Performing Content 28

  The Content Template...................................28

  Writing Great Content..................................30

Summary...35

  Your Content Toolbox 35

Search Engine Optimization (SEO).....................**39**

Technical SEO 40

  1. Identify Crawl Errors 40

  2. Mobile Usability 41

  3. Page Speed 41

4. Site Security (HTTPS) 43

On-Page SEO...44

Step 1: Prioritizing On-Page SEO Efforts 44

Step 2: Page-Level SEO Research 50

Step 3: On-Page Optimization 51

Off-Page SEO 56

Link Building 56

Social Media 58

Online PR 58

Summary...60

Your SEO Toolbox 60

Digital Advertising (PPC) 63

Establishing a Budget 63

Choosing Digital Advertising Networks 64

Facebook Ads 65

Audience 66

Ad Delivery Types 66

Costs...67

Facebook Ads Strategy 68

Audience 68

Content (Ads)..69

Google Ads 72

Audience 73

Ad Delivery Types 73

Ad Extensions 74

Costs..75

Google Ads Strategy 75

Keywords 76

Content (Ads)..81

Landing Pages 83

Other Ad Networks..84

Summary...86

Your Digital Advertising Toolbox..86

Social Media..89

Choosing the Right Social Networks..89

Building Your Social Media Audience...91

Using Social Media to Drive Website Traffic 92

Posting More - A *Lot* More..92

Make Your Content Easy to Share...97

Become a Trusted Curator of Content 98

Summary...100

Your Social Media Toolbox..100

Resources...103

Content Audit Template 104

Content Research Template..108

Content Production Template 112

Clickthrough Rate Opportunities..116

Google Ads Keyword Research...118

Introduction

When I set out to write this book, I wanted to produce a blueprint for business owners, entrepreneurs, and marketers to grow their website traffic significantly. I'm not talking about incremental growth over time. I'm talking about big gains.

That's why my goal is for you to double your traffic. If you have an established website and you follow the steps in this book, I fully believe this is possible. If you're just getting started or have a newer website with very little traffic - I want you to aim bigger. We don't want to double 50 visitors a month. We want to 5x, 10x or 20x that number.

Let me clarify one thing before you begin: Increasing website traffic is not the *only* goal that will lead you to business success online. Most individuals and organizations are (and should be) focused on lead generation, sales, conversion rate, etc. All of these measurables are hugely important, but they generally don't happen without a steady stream of high-quality, relevant traffic coming to your website. Once you finish this book, put your strategy in place, and begin to implement these tactics, I highly recommend turning your attention to those meaningful goals.

So, why listen to me? I've spent nearly 15 years focused on creating digital marketing strategies that drive results for organizations. I spent nearly ten years working on the organizational side where I tripled website growth year-over-year. My desire to work with businesses of all shapes and sizes led me to my current career as the Vice President of Digital Marketing for one of Cleveland's top web agencies. I work with companies big and small in all industries, and I've fine-tuned my strategies so they can be tailored to any website.

If you follow all of the principles in this book, you will see your website traffic grow over time. If you're looking for specific tactics and strategies in the areas of content marketing, search engine optimization, digital advertising, or social media, you'll find a wealth in this book. Lastly, inside, you'll find a packed toolbox of digital marketing tools that I've used to generate huge gains in website traffic.

Enjoy the book and don't forget to check out **theDoubleBook.com** for additional resources.

Content Marketing

This is the first chapter because frankly, it's the foundation of your strategy. If you're going to double your website traffic, great content is going to be at the core of your effort. Here are a few statistics that show why content marketing is so important:

- Year-over-year growth in unique site traffic is **7.8x higher** for content marketing leaders compared to followers (19.7% vs. 2.5%). *(Source: Aberdeen)*
- Businesses publishing 16-plus posts a month get almost **3.5 times more traffic** than businesses publishing zero to four articles. *(Source: Hubspot)*
- Companies that blog have **434% more indexed pages** than businesses without blogs. *(Source: Hubspot)*

There are three stages we're going to work through to maximize your content marketing efforts:

- Content Audit
- Content Strategy
- Content Production

Content Audit

Before you map out a content strategy that will drive quality traffic, you need to get a sense of where you're at today. I routinely use the following exercise for auditing existing site content in preparation for developing a content strategy.

Keep, Update, Combine, Delete

One of my favorite exercises when it comes to auditing content is the **Keep, Update, Combine, Delete** exercise. The process is exactly as the name sounds. Here's how to get started:

1. **Start with your spreadsheet tool of choice.** My two favorites are Google Sheets and Microsoft Excel.
2. **Export Pages and Analytics from Google Analytics.** It's critical to see how each page is performing, so I like to look at metrics like *organic pageviews*, which is the number of pageviews from search traffic. I like to look at a 6-12 month window of time when looking at this data, and I always export this from Google Analytics.

Exporting Data from Google Analytics

Pulling the website data you'll need for this exercise is as simple as following a few steps:

1. Log in to Google Analytics.
2. Navigate to **Behavior > Site Content > All Pages**.
3. Change the time frame (upper right-hand corner) to the past 6-12 months.

4. Click the **Export** link (upper right-hand corner) and choose either Google Sheets or Excel, depending on which platform you're using.

You're going to want to simplify this data by removing all of the columns except for the **Page** and **Pageviews**. We'll then add a new column named "Status."

Note: Sometimes, Google Analytics data can be messy. You may have additional information on your URLs called "query strings" that make assessing the total pageviews for each page challenging. You'll know this if some of your URLs have a question mark at the end of the URL, followed by additional data. Don't worry; I've put together an exclusive handy guide to cleaning up this information that you can access here: *thedoublebook.com/content-cleanup*.

Example Spreadsheet

URL	Pageviews	Status
https://www.yoursite.com/page	515	
https://www.yoursite.com/blog-post	215	
https://www.yoursite.com/about-page	205	
https://www.yoursite.com/product-post	75	

I like to sort this spreadsheet by pageviews to start with the highest-traffic pages first (Pageviews highest-to-lowest). Then, as the name of the exercise implies, we're going to go page-by-page and categorize them as **Keep, Combine, Update,** or **Delete.** I've added several template pages for you to use in the Resources section near the back of this book.

Here are some simple rules of thumb to help you through the process:

1. **Keep.** These are the pages that have up-to-date content and are generally driving a good amount of page views. They're still highly relevant and aren't duplicating content from any other pages on your site.

2. **Combine.** Use this category when you have multiple pages focused on the same topic. Likely more common with blog posts, if you wrote about the same topic multiple times and one of these posts is driving the majority of the pageviews, consider combining the other post(s) with the top-performing post. (Don't forget to add 301 redirects from any pages that you delete)

3. **Update.** As the name implies, out-of-date pages would be classified as "Update" pages. For the core pages on your site, focus on up-to-date information with strong visuals and video if possible. As you go back through your blog archive, you'll likely come across posts that are no longer accurate or complete. These are great pieces of content to update. I'll show you how to update these pages in this chapter and the next chapter on SEO.

4. **Delete.** This category is reserved for unsalvageable content. It's typically content that's irrelevant, outdated, and low-performing. You'll find better candidates for this category toward the bottom of your spreadsheet where pages are receiving limited or no pageviews.

You might be wondering, "Why am I deleting content if I'm trying to *grow* traffic to my website?" It's a fair question.

First, your goal is to reduce the amount of low-quality pages that have thin content and low engagement. You're simply eliminating pages and blog posts that aren't performing well already, and favoring quality over quantity.

Second, you're eliminating the risk of keyword cannibalization. You might be picturing Hannibal Lecter, but in reality, keyword cannibalization occurs when multiple pages are vying for traffic focused on the same keyword or keywords. When this happens, your own site's pages are competing against themselves for search engine exposure. That's why we **Combine** or **Delete** content.

Content Audit Next Steps

Once you've completed the exercise, celebrate. Eat a cupcake or find someone to high-five. After you come down from the endorphin high of a quality high-five, it's time to get to work.

Depending on the amount of **Combine** and **Update** pages you have, you may want to spread this work out over a few months or even a year. Here are some tips for developing a strategy to tackle content after your audit:

1. **Prioritize.** You may not be able to complete everything on this list, and that's ok. You're going for big wins. That means you must focus on content that already has a high volume of traffic, or content that is essential to your business. I'll also show you how to identify high-opportunity SEO pages in the next chapter.

2. **Clean house.** One of the easiest (and most satisfying) actions to take is to remove all of the "Delete" content. Make sure that you're setting up 301 redirects to appropriate pages when you delete these. 301 redirects tell search engines where traffic to a deleted page should go. If you're using Wordpress, you can use a plugin like *Simple 301 Redirects* to accomplish this. You may notice a temporary dip in traffic for a few weeks after this, but if you've done this right, that wouldn't have been quality traffic in the first place.

3. **Plan and Delegate.** If you have a lot of content, you can't do this alone. Enlist in the help of colleagues or freelancers (Fiverr, Upwork, and Lowpost are some of my favorites) to help you work through updating and combining content. Assign dates by which you want each piece of content to be updated. Later in this chapter, we'll introduce the idea of a content calendar and the tools you can use to build one.

Content Strategy

Remember, as we stated before, we're focused on quality content over quantity. But if you're going to double your website traffic in a year, you're going to need to focus on creating *as much* new quality content as possible. That means having a plan. Here are the key steps to building a successful content strategy:

1. Choose Your Topics
2. Topic Validation: Perform SEO Research
3. Topic Selection: Choosing the Right Topics by Focusing on High Volume, Low Competition Keywords
4. Plan and Write Your Content (or Outsource It!)

Choose Your Topics

Choosing content topics is an art and a science. It takes a strong qualitative understanding of your audience, their needs, desires, challenges, and goals. It also takes strong quantitative research to ensure that you're focusing on topics that are in-demand and specific enough not to get lost in an overly-competitive landscape.

Topic Ideation

So how do you come up with ideas and topics for producing new content? For many individuals, this is the hardest part of developing content. It's much harder to stare at a blank piece of paper or screen than one that has a prompt. Don't worry, here are some of the tried-and-true ways I've been able to generate dozens of topic ideas within just one working session:

- **Top Sales Questions** - Asking your sales team the most common questions they receive during the sales process is one of my favorite sources of content ideas. List the top ten, twenty, or even fifty ideas that you get. If you don't have a sales team, talk to whoever interacts with prospects, leads, and customers. You want to get as close to the frontline as you can.
- **Competitors** - Check out your competitors' websites and research the topics about which they're writing. Can you take a different angle, or write a better version of what they've produced? Two of my favorite tools to view competitors' top content are SEMRush and SpyFu.
- **Industry Trends** - Jot down some of the biggest trends affecting your industry. Visit industry association websites or blogs to identify the topics about which they're writing. Check

out any relevant LinkedIn industry Groups and identify which discussions have the most engagement.

- **Ubersuggest** – A great free tool that allows you to enter a seed keyword and retrieve popular content that has already been published, including each post's number of backlinks and social shares.

- **Answer the Public** - One of my very favorite tools, Answer the Public allows you to put in a keyword and identify the top questions that are commonly asked on search engines related to that topic. Document the ones that align with your audience. The free version of this tool is great, but the paid version will give you unlimited searches and data that you can't see in the free version.

Topic Validation

Now that you have a good list of topics, it's time to validate your ideas. In other words, we've done the qualitative work - now we need to do the quantitative work.

For this part of your content strategy, I recommend creating another spreadsheet that will help you work through the process. Here's how I recommend setting it up:

Topic	Target Keyword	Search Volume	Keyword Difficulty

From here, list all of your topic ideas in the first column. Next, we want to identify a target keyword, keywords, or keyphrase to research. Sometimes this can be easy because it's right in the topic idea itself.

For example, if your topic is "How do I increase traffic to my website?", you might choose a keyphrase like "increase website traffic."

For some topics, identifying target keywords will be less clear-cut. If you're researching "Using Content and SEO to increase website traffic," there are a lot more options. You could try "content increase website traffic," "SEO increase website traffic," and many other variations with more or less words.

Exercise: Performing Topic Keyword Research

To properly evaluate each of your topic ideas, you're going to want to get a sense of how much search volume there is for your target keyword(s) and how difficult it will be to rank for those keywords. Here are some of my favorite tools to do this research:

1. **SEMRush** - Top of this list because you can quite literally drop in your list of keywords, let the tool do the digging, and have all of the data at your fingertips within minutes.
2. **KeySearch** - A lower-cost alternative to SEMRush that will require more manual search of each of your keywords. In addition to keyword research, KeySearch has been building out a ton of great features for SEO and Content research.
3. **WordTracker** - Another great, lower-cost tool focused on keyword research.
4. **SpyFu** - Similar to SEMRush, this tool is more robust and focused on SEO and PPC research. If you're looking for a more full-featured research tool, this one of my favorites.

Once you've researched each of the topics and keywords on your list, you should have a completed spreadsheet that looks something like this:

Topic	Target Keyword	Search Volume	Keyword Difficulty
How to use Pinterest to drive traffic to your website	Pinterest marketing	880	46
What are the fastest ways to increase traffic to your website?	how to drive traffic to your website	880	45
What are the elements of a good blog post?	How to write a blog	8100	51

Topic Selection: Choosing the Right Topics by Focusing on High Volume, Low Competition Keywords

To double your website traffic, you need to focus on high-opportunity content topics. That means you can't start by focusing on keywords like "shoes." You need to focus on *longtail keywords* that often have multiple words and are very specific. In this scenario, you might instead target "women's shoes for long-distance running."

You're going to look at your spreadsheet and identify some high-opportunity topics - those with high volume and low competition. When I refer to competition, this is going to be a metric of how saturated the search results are and how hard it will be to rank quickly for this keyword. Each keyword research tool may have a slightly different term for this, whether it be "keyword difficulty," "competition," or something else.

When looking for these high volume, low competition keywords, this is going to be completely relative to *your* research. Some of you may find that most of your keywords are in the hundreds to low-thousands in terms of monthly search volume. Others may be operating in an industry or niche where there's much more search volume.

Here are some helpful tips for identifying your best opportunities:

- **Avoid the ends of the Search Volume spectrum** - You should avoid keywords and topics that have very low volume, generally in the single and double digits in terms of searches per month. You won't be able to get enough traction here. You'll also likely be avoiding keywords/topics that have very high search volume, for example, 100,000 monthly searches or above. At this end of the spectrum, it's likely going to be too competitive to rank quickly.
- **Dive deeper** - If you think you have a good opportunity with decent volume and moderate-to-low competition, run a Google search for that keyword. If the search results are fairly shallow and you believe you can produce better content than what you see on the first and second page of search results, it's likely a good opportunity!
- **Leverage keyword recommendations** - Most of the keyword research tools mentioned before will also give you additional keyword recommendations based on the keyword you're researching. Take a look at those and see if the recommendations produce a variation with even more search volume or lower competition.

During the topic selection process, you're not looking for perfection. You're looking to prioritize a certain number of topics that you can write about throughout the year. If you plan on writing one piece of content per month, you will need to prioritize the top twelve topics from your research. Alternately, if you plan on producing content weekly, you'll need 50+ topics in your bank.

30-Day Challenge:
Plan an Entire Year's Worth of Content

Here's your first challenge, and it's a great one to start early in the year! Using the strategies outlined above, build a spreadsheet (or use a content calendar tool) to build out *one full year* of content for your website or blog.

Each piece of content should have a target keyword, search volume, and keyword difficulty. Assign who's going to write each piece of content and pencil in a publish date. Print this out, share it with others, and you'll be much more likely to stick to your content plan!

Plan and Write Your Content (or Outsource It!)

Once you have your high-opportunity content topics identified, it's a good idea to put a plan together for the year. Most people use a content calendar, and the good news is that you already have the beginning of a calendar built with your topic spreadsheet. All you need to do is add a column or two for Writer and Publish Date.

Topic	Target Keyword	Search Volume	Keyword Difficulty	Writer	Publish Date
How to use Pinterest to drive traffic to your website	Pinterest marketing	880	46		
What are the fastest ways to increase traffic to your website?	how to drive traffic to your website	880	45		
What are the elements of a good blog post?	How to write a blog	8100	51		

If you want to get fancier or more efficient, there are plenty of content calendar tools out there to leverage, including Trello (free) and DivvyHQ.

Once you've completed your content calendar, you should have a full year (or length of time of your choosing) worth of content ideas that have been identified as excellent opportunities.

Now, who's going to write this? If you're like most people (entrepreneurs, business owners, marketers, etc.), it's hard to imagine producing all of this content. You're going to need some help, so here are a few ideas to get you started:

1. **Enlist Colleagues** - If you work within an organization, you likely have a few colleagues who have expertise in some of the topic areas you've chosen. Get them excited about the opportunity to double your website traffic and become a published web author!

2. **Outsource** - Many years ago, it would have been challenging to find a freelance writer with experience in your specific niche or industry at an affordable rate. Today, you can do just that. Here are a few of my favorite platforms for finding affordable freelance writers:

   a. **Upwork** - A huge pool of freelancers and the ability to sort by experience, hourly rate, credentials, and more make this my favorite platform to find great content writers.

   b. **LowPost** - This platform is focused solely and content, and you can find writers that will not only produce content but help you with content strategy as well.

   c. **Fiverr** – This is the most cost-effective platform on this list, but also the widest-ranging in terms of quality. I would stay away from the introductory $5 blog posts, but you can certainly find credentialed writers that can produce a quality piece of content for $100 or less.

So there you have it. At this point, you should have an excellent sense of the existing content on your site and a complete plan and strategy for your content for the next year. Now it's time to dive into some tips for writing high-performing content that will rank in search engines and drive visitors to your site.

How to Write High-Performing Content

This is where we're going to start to see the huge overlap between Content and SEO. While some SEO techniques don't necessarily require content, most of the highly-effective ones do.

The Content Template

I use a consistent template that has all of the critical elements that I feel are important for a high-performing piece of content. Here's what it looks like:

Page/Blog Post Title:	
Meta Title:	Meta Description:
Target Keyword:	Secondary Keywords:
LSI Keywords:	
Questions:	
Internal Links:	External Links:

Before putting even one word into the content itself, I recommend filling this out completely. You can find blank templates near the back of the book in the Resources section. Since you've already done the topic research and keyword research, it shouldn't take too long. Let's dive into each one of these.

Page/Blog Post Title

Since you've already put together your content calendar, you should have a topic already. Now we need to write a high-quality title. Focus on a title that is actionable, intriguing, or empathetic. Try to include your target SEO keyword(s) in the title. Experiment with adding numbers for lists and strong adjectives to make your title more compelling.

Meta Title

This title is displayed in search engine results pages. Try to keep it under 50-60 characters and include one or two important keywords towards the beginning of the title.

Meta Description

This description is displayed in search engine results pages under the meta title. Try to keep it under 160 characters and write compelling copy to draw readers into your page. It's important to note that Meta Description is no longer a Google ranking factor, so you should focus on a description that inspires searchers to click on your search result rather than focusing too much on SEO.

Target Keyword

You should have already identified a target keyword through your research, and you can even include search volume and keyword difficulty in this section if you like.

Secondary Keywords

Identify additional related keywords or keyphrases to include in your content. Use free tools like KeywordTool.io and Infinite Suggest to gather ideas. If you need unlimited searches or more functionality, you can use tools like SEMRush, KeySearch, or Wordtracker.

LSI Keywords

LSI stands for Latent Semantic Indexing. Think of LSI keywords as related terms. For example, someone searching for "peanut butter" may be looking for "recipes," "peanut butter and jelly," "allergies," etc. It's important to understand these keywords as they provide context into what users are looking for when they search for a topic. My favorite tool by far is LSIGraph (free version limited to 3 searches per day), but KeySearch will give you some decent data as well.

Questions

I mentioned before one of my favorite tools is *Answer the Public*. This tool will allow you to see all of the common questions asked around a specific keyword. The important thing here is that you understand what questions the user is asking, so you can answer them in your content.

Internal Links

When thinking about rapidly increasing site traffic, one of the valuable things that you can do is to create a robust internal link network within your site. In your content template, document a few pages on your site to which you might link. Think about relevant product or service pages or other blog posts that have related content.

External Links

A valuable piece of content often has links to reputable external sites as well. Not only does this give your content more credibility, but it also sends signals to search engines that can improve a page or site's authority. I generally recommend 2-3 high-quality, reputable outbound links when possible.

Writing Great Content

There are 2.5 million blog posts published every day. Every. Day. That means you're up against some pretty stiff competition. If you've done your homework and identified solid topics, performed keyword research, and completed the content template, you likely already have an advantage over the majority of that content. To take it to the next level, you need to focus on writing not just good content, but great content.

Always Keep the User in Mind

Keep your content template handy and you should be able to get in the mind of the user easily. What questions do they have about this topic? What are some of the related issues that should be covered? Google and other search engines reward content that matches the user's search intent. As a result, if your piece of content is *the best* result for a specific search query, it has a good chance of performing well in search.

If your content doesn't address the user's needs, it will likely result in a high bounce rate. High bounce rates send a signal to search engines that the content isn't useful for users, and will result in poor performance.

Write Naturally

Gone are the days of stuffing as many SEO keywords into your content as possible. Point blank, you will either get penalized for this or see poor performance because it will read like a robot wrote it. Instead, get back to basics and write for *humans*. Depending on your organization's tone, you may be able to write more conversationally.

Yes, you want to do your best to use your primary and secondary keywords in your content, but only in a natural way.

Focus on Actionable Takeaways

A high-performing piece of content gives the user value. When I started writing this book, I knew I couldn't just write at a very high-level without giving examples or resources. That's why I decided to share the step-by-step processes and tools that I use every day. Don't make readers go elsewhere to find what they're looking for - give it to them the first time.

Format for Readability

One of the increasingly important signals that search engines look at when indexing pages is usability. That means if your site isn't mobile-friendly, has a poor design, or is hard to read, your content is going to be devalued. Formatting content for better readability is as simple as following a few tips:

- **Leverage headers** - Use headers (H1, H2, H3, etc.) to not only categorize the hierarchy of your information for search engines but also to help readers navigate from section to section.
- **Use lists** - Bulleted and numbered lists are an *excellent* way to break up large walls of content, and they make information significantly more scannable.
- **Use strong visuals** - If your web page or blog post is absent of visuals, it's hard to break up large chunks of written content. Use stock images from free sites like Unsplash or Pexels, or paid sites like iStockPhoto or Adobe Stock. Better yet, create custom imagery like infographics - a great task to outsource to a talented designer on Fiverr.

- **Write short paragraphs.** Paragraphs with too many sentences are just hard to read. I recommend paragraphs of 3-5 sentences when possible.

Consider Content Length

If you do a quick search for "ideal blog post length," you're going to find some strong opinions on both ends of the spectrum. Here are some good rules of thumb that I've used in my experience:

- For product/service/organization pages, don't focus on length, focus on providing the *best* information. Do your research, answer user questions, provide as many resources as you can, and leave it at that. Your page might be 200 words or 2,000 words.
- For blog posts, I have *generally* found that longer posts (1,000-2,000+ words) *tend* to perform better. BUT, and there's a big caveat here, I don't believe longer content performs better because it's *longer*. I believe it tends to perform better because it's more thorough and does a better job of meeting the user's needs.

Bonus Tool:
Grammarly

For anyone writing content, especially those without a writing background, Grammarly is a lifesaver. Grammarly automatically detects grammar, spelling, punctuation, word choice, and style mistakes in your writing. Grammarly is available as a plugin for Google Chrome, Firefox, Microsoft Edge, and Safari, and you can also use the editor directly on the site (grammarly.com). Best of all - it's free!

Summary

Content is at the epicenter of your journey to double your website traffic. It is entirely possible to create massive long-term growth through content production alone. I've seen this time-and-time again with companies that deeply understand their audience and commit to regularly posting high-quality content. You'll see in the next chapter how tightly-connected Content and SEO are.

Your Content Toolbox

Content Research

- **Google Analytics** - The best free all-around analytics platform out there. Use it to pull pageview data during your content audit. *(Free version suitable for most users; Google Analytics 360 for enterprise customers)*
- **Microsoft Excel / Google Sheets** - Spreadsheet software that we're using to combine and consolidate website data and analytics during our content audit. *(Office 365 - $69.99/year; Google Sheets - free)*

Keyword/SEO Research

- **SEMRush** - My vote for the best all-around SEO platform for the money. In this chapter, we're using SEMRush to perform keyword research, generate topic ideas, perform competitive research, and more. *(Starts at $99/month)*
- **Ubersuggest** – A free tool for researching keywords and content.

- **Answer the Public** - The best tool for identifying questions that users ask related to a specific keyword. *(Free with limitations; Pro version - $99/year)*
- **KeySearch** - My pick for the best low-cost alternative to more expensive SEO suites. A great tool for keyword and topic research.
- **WordTracker** - Another cost-effective alternative to more expensive SEO suites, focused on SEO and PPC research. *(Starts at $27/month)*
- **SpyFu** - SEO tool specifically focused on paid and organic research; great for competitor research. *(Starts at $39/month)*
- **KeywordTool.io** – A great tool for getting autocomplete suggestions from search engines in bulk, and great for generating keyword ideas. *(Free version is probably enough for most users; Pro starts at $89/month)*
- **Infinite Suggest** - Another great (and free) tool for autocomplete suggestions from search engines.
- **LSIGraph** – This is my absolute favorite tool to generate LSI (latent semantic index) keywords. Think "related" keywords. *(3 free searches per day; Paid version starts at $27/month and is worth the money)*

Content Production

- **Fiverr** - The lowest cost way to access designers, writers, and creative freelancers to help with content production. Quality varies, so look for a freelancer with good reviews, and avoid the $5 projects.
- **Upwork** - A much higher-quality network for outsourcing projects and finding freelancers. *(Cost varies based on experience, but generally $25-100/hour)*

- **Lowpost** - Another vetted network of freelance writers that can also assist with content strategy. I find the prices to be more affordable than Upwork. *(100-word content starts at $19)*
- **Trello** - A great, free way to organize content topics or a content calendar.
- **DivvyHQ** – A more robust content marketing platform, complete with a content calendar, idea storage and content repository, project management, and more. *(Starts at $39/month)*
- **Unsplash** - My pick for the best free stock image site. Photojournalistic, high-resolution images, and an ever-growing library.
- **Pexels** - Another free stock image site very similar to Unsplash. I almost always use both when looking for stock photos.
- **iStockPhoto** – A paid stock images site. The benefit is a huge library, but you must subscribe or pay for every image individually.
- **Adobe Stock** - Very similar to iStockPhoto is Adobe's stock images site. Also has a huge library and a very similar pricing model.

Search Engine Optimization (SEO)

Since we just dove deep into content, it's only appropriate for us to move on to SEO (search engine optimization). As I previously mentioned, there's almost no way to talk about SEO without talking about content in some way.

When approaching SEO for a website, I typically segment it into three categories: technical, on-page, and off-page. When speaking with others, I almost always use the analogy of a three-legged stool, with each of these categories acting as one of the legs. And we all know what happens to a stool when one leg is missing.

Technical SEO is going to set the foundation for ensuring that search engines find your site and its content. On-page SEO ensures that the content on your site ranks well for the right topics. Finally, off-page SEO leverages the value of other sites that send valuable signals to search engines about the credibility of your site.

Technical SEO

Technical SEO is one area that certainly scares off most non-SEO professionals. "Technical" implies that this work is going to be complex; however, that's not always the case. While you may need some design or development help along the way, there are several things you can do independently to positively impact performance.

As you'll notice throughout this section, one of my very favorite tools for running an in-depth technical SEO audit is *SEMRush*. While I haven't used it, I've also heard and read excellent things about *Deep Crawl* from many industry professionals.

For much of this section, I also recommend using Google Search Console. If you're not already using Google Search Console, setting it up is simple, and you can access it for free here:

search.google.com/search-console

1. Identify Crawl Errors

Identifying crawl errors is a great place to start because you can see if there are any issues with search engines' ability to crawl your site. A great tool to get a snapshot of any crawl errors is the "Coverage" report within Google Search Console (formerly Google Webmaster Tools).

Common errors that are found here are 404 errors (page not found) and issues with your site's robots.txt file (tells search engines how to crawl your site). If you identify any issues, you'll likely want to work with a developer (or Google your way through troubleshooting) to resolve these errors.

2. Mobile Usability

Point blank, if your website isn't optimized for mobile devices these days, it will not perform well in search. Google rolled out its "Mobile-First Index," which means when it crawls your site, it's crawling the *mobile* version of your site. If your site is not mobile-friendly, you will see decreased performance.

Within Google Search Console, the Mobile Usability report will show you any errors and issues, including text that is too small to read, buttons that are too hard to tap, and content that is wider than the viewport. Identifying these issues and resolving them should be essential items on your to-do list.

3. Page Speed

When was the last time you patiently waited 5-10 seconds for a page to load? Odds are (and based on loads of research), you didn't. You left and went to a competitor's site. Not only is that bad for *your* website, it's a bad experience for the user. Because of that, search engines like Google are taking notice, and penalizing sites and pages that take a long time to load.

Google has built a very handy tool called PageSpeed Insights that allows you to enter a URL and receive recommendations on speeding up that page. You'll first see a performance score from 0 to 100 (0 being slow, 100 being fast). Further down on the page, you'll see specific recommendations for improving that page's performance.

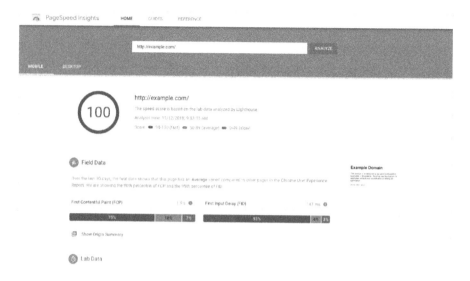

Google Page Speed Insights

Here are some of the most common page speed issues and how to solve them:

- **Compress images** - Huge, high-resolution images are often a biggest contributor to a slow page. Resolving this doesn't mean your site has to feature small, low-resolution photos, though. If you're using Wordpress, install an image compression tool like WP Smush Image. Compress JPEG is another free tool that allows you to quickly and easily compress images without losing a ton of quality.

- **Leverage browser caching** - Every time a web page loads, a slew of resources (content, images, javascript, styles, etc.) need to be fetched from a server. Browser caching is a method of allowing some of these resources to be saved on a user's device so the next time they visit, every *individual* resource doesn't need to load. Browser caching can have a huge impact on page load speed. For Wordpress sites, check out W3 Total Cache.

For non-Wordpress sites, you'll likely want to speak with a developer about leveraging browser caching.

- **Minify HTML** - When HTML code is written, there is often a lot of unused and duplicated code, as well as space used for formatting that can be removed ("minimized"). HTML Minifier is a great tool for this and gives you a lot of flexibility and options. HTMLMinifier (same name, different tool) runs server-side, which means you don't need to minify HTML each time it's edited, but you'll also likely need a developer for implementation.

4. Site Security (HTTPS)

Site security is another hugely important signal for Google. This one is pretty simple. If your site is not secure (if the URL starts with http://...), then you need to secure it with an SSL certificate. A few *very* important things to keep in mind *(warning: wandering into technical territory)*:

- When you do this, *ensure* that all of the internal links within your site are updated to "https" links, which can be done with the help of a database "search and replace."
- Ensure that all references to scripts, style sheets, images, etc. are also updated to "https" using the same technique.
- Ensure canonical tags point to "https" URL versions.
- Force "https" with redirects.
- Update sitemaps.
- Update robots.txt file with a new sitemap.
- Update Google Analytics and Google Search Console to reflect the new "https" version of your site.

This list certainly isn't exhaustive, but it's a good reference to use or share with your developer.

On-Page SEO

From my experience, technical SEO forms the critical foundation for ensuring that your site can be found. I like to clear out as many technical SEO issues as early as possible and then move on. On-page SEO is where you can really boost traffic, and with a little instruction, anyone can do it.

Before you begin, it's important to note that SEO doesn't impact traffic overnight. It's common not to see the results of certain optimizations for three to six months or more. Prioritizing and monitoring will be critical to your SEO success.

Step 1: Prioritizing On-Page SEO Efforts

Keeping in mind the goal of doubling your website traffic, prioritizing SEO efforts is critical. We're going for big wins rather than lots of small victories. Here are some of my criteria for finding these big opportunities:

- Finding pages that are targeting high volume, low competition keywords.
- Finding pages that are already performing well for high-volume keywords with room for improvement.
- Finding pages that may be ranking well, but are not receiving the traffic expected for their position in search results.

I use several proven strategies for identifying the best SEO opportunities at any given time. Let me share some of my favorites:

1. Finding Big Opportunities with SEMRush

Within SEMRush's Organic Research tool (paid), enter your website URL and look at the *Positions* section of the report. This report will show you every single keyword for which your site ranks. Here are the exact search parameters I use to narrow down the best opportunities:

- **Sort by Volume (highest to lowest)** - We want to optimize for keywords that have high search volume.
- **Volume Greater Than 100** - Any keywords that yield less than 100 searches per month won't provide you with the big wins that you need.
- **Top 50 Positions** - This allows us to see pages that are already ranking within the top 5 pages of Google results.
- **Keyword Difficulty Less than 80%** - This threshold can be played with, but the key here is that we're looking for keywords that aren't incredibly competitive.

Just using these simple filters, you should now have a list of keywords and their associated pages that present great opportunities for optimization that can result in big traffic gains. I recommend exporting this report as an Excel file and saving it for later.

2. Using Google Search Console to Identify Rank Improvement Opportunities

If you don't have a tool like SEMRush (if you're serious about SEO, you should) then Google Search Console can still provide you with an immense amount of valuable data. I like to identify pages that are already receiving significant search *exposure*, but have opportunities to show up even higher in search results. Here's the step-by-step:

1. Within Google Search Console, access the *Search Results* report from the left-hand navigation.

2. I like to choose a timeframe of roughly the last six months.
3. Ensure that you click the area labeled "Average Position" so this metric shows up in your results as well.
4. In the results below the graph, click on the *Pages* tab.
5. Click on *Impressions* in the table header to sort by Search Impressions from high-to-low.

You're now looking at all of the pages on your site during the last six months, sorted by the number of impressions they've received.

The goal is to identify high-impression pages that are ranking anywhere between the 5th and 20th position. After position 5, there's a dropoff in clickthrough rate, and these results are likely to be "below the fold." After position 10, these site pages are going to be ranked on the second page of search results, resulting in a continued dropoff in clickthrough rate.

There are two ways you can use this data:

1. You can browse through this data and note or document pages near the top of this list (higher search volume) that rank between positions 5 and 20.
2. Even better, you can export all of this data to a spreadsheet and apply filters to only include pages ranking between 5 and 20. Then sort by Impressions highest-to-lowest, and you have a pretty good list in priority order.

Using this list, you now have a second source of on-page SEO opportunities.

3. Using Google Search Console to Identify Clickthrough Rate Opportunities

One of the reasons I don't like getting too hung up on rankings is that it's only half the battle. Once your page is ranked for a quality keyword, the user still needs to *click* on your page in the search results. Generally, pages that are ranked higher, especially on the first page, see higher clickthrough rates.

Here are average clickthrough rates by position according to Advanced Web Ranking:

Position	Clickthrough Rate (Desktop)	Clickthrough Rate (Mobile)
1	30.71%	23.08%
2	15.46%	13.82%
3	9.60%	9.55%
4	6.16%	7.25%
5	4.17%	7.50%
6	2.95%	3.43%
7	2.16%	2.30%
8	1.66%	1.82%
9	1.34%	1.41%
10	1.10%	1.08%

After you get past the first page, the clickthrough rate on desktop is between 1-2%, and mobile is slightly less than 1%.

So how do we use this data? We use Google Search Console data to find pages that have a lower clickthrough rate than expected. Here's how:

1. Within Google Search Console, access the *Search Results* report from the left-hand navigation.
2. I like to choose a timeframe of roughly the last six months.
3. Ensure that you click the areas labeled "Average CTR" and "Average Position" so these metrics show up in your results as well.
4. In the results below the graph, click on the *Pages* tab.
5. Click on *Impressions* in the table header to sort by Search Impressions from high-to-low.

You're once again looking at all of the pages on your site during the last six months, sorted by the number of impressions they've received. I'd recommend exporting this data for future use.

The goal is to look at high-impression pages, especially those ranking in positions one through ten, and identify the ones that have an Average CTR lower than the industry average in the previous table based on Average Position. Here's an example:

URL	Average CTR (Search Console)	Average Position	Average CTR (Reference)
https://www.yoursite.com/page	2.06%	5.1	4.17%
https://www.yoursite.com/blog-post	1.08%	9.9	1.1%
https://www.yoursite.com/service	2.75%	6.5	2.16%

In this example, I've found a page that, during my selected time period of six months, has had an average position of 5.1 - essentially, the fifth position. It's clickthrough rate during that time, though, has been 2.06%, significantly lower than the average for the fifth position. *This is an opportunity.*

Document all of the pages that fit this criteria of underperforming pages, as we'll use it as a third source of on-page SEO opportunities.

Bonus Tool:
Animalz Revive

I recently discovered this tool from Animalz, a content marketing agency. Just link up your Google Analytics account and Revive will find content that has been decaying, or losing traffic. These are terrific opportunities to reassess page content and optimize these pages.

Step 2: Page-Level SEO Research

Every page on your site should have one or multiple target keywords. I'm not a big advocate of getting *too* focused on *one single keyword*, because that isn't how search works these days, but it's important to have a general sense of the keywords and topics for which you're hoping to rank.

Revisit the *Performing Topic Keyword Research* exercise we performed in the Content chapter for a refresher. Here's the template I recommend using for research on every new page or post you write or optimize:

Page/Blog Post Title:	
Meta Title:	Meta Description:
Target Keyword:	Secondary Keywords:
LSI Keywords:	
Questions:	
Internal Links:	External Links:

Step 3: On-Page Optimization

Content

While you're going to spend some time optimizing metadata and other technical aspects of the page, the most important on-page optimization you can make is updating the content. I highly recommend referencing the section on "How to Write High-Performing Content" in the first chapter to ensure that each page's content is optimized for both humans and search engines.

Meta Titles and Descriptions

Some digital marketers will classify this type of optimization as technical SEO, but for me, meta titles and descriptions really come down to *content* research and optimization.

Meta Titles

Still one of the most critical elements of a page when it comes to SEO, meta titles are displayed in search results as the clickable headline for a given page. Here are a few tips for optimizing each meta title:

- Keep your titles to under 60 characters to ensure that they'll fully display in search results.

- Ensure that each page has a unique meta title. Duplicate meta titles are confusing for search engines and are often flagged by SEO audit tools.

- Use your target keyword or phrase somewhere in the first half of the title.

- Use keywords naturally, and don't stuff your meta title. Your title should read clearly and not simply list all target keywords or repeat keywords.

- If you're going to use your brand name, use it consistently. If your brand name is recognizable, including it can boost rankings or clickthrough rate. Brand names are commonly added at the end of the meta title after a dash ("-") or a pipe ("|").

Meta Descriptions

Meta descriptions provide a brief description of a page in search results. To dispel a common misconception, meta descriptions are *not* a ranking factor for Google. That means you can stuff as many keywords as your heart desires into a meta description; it won't help your ranking. Instead, meta descriptions are an *incredibly* valuable tool for increasing clickthrough rates from search results pages.

Here are some recommendations for optimizing each page's meta description:

- Limit meta descriptions to 160 characters, but try to use as much of that character count as you can when writing your description.

- Write a compelling description. Remember, this, along with your meta title, is the primary content shown to users in search results. Think about your audience and target keywords when writing your description. Make it actionable if possible.
- Use target keywords naturally. When your meta description contains a keyword that was used in the user's search query, Google will bold that keyword, making your description stand out. Don't unnaturally stuff all of your target keywords in your description, but where natural, include them.

To The Web has a great "Test Page Title & Meta Description Visibility" tool to preview meta title and meta description together to ensure they fit within Google's character and pixel limits.

URL

The URL of a page still does have some minor SEO value for search engines. The value of a properly-optimized URL lies more in indicating to a user the content and intent on a page. Let's look at the example below:

www.cameras.com/nikon/d500-dx-4k-camera

In this example, there is a lot of information that can benefit both search engines and users. In addition to a brand name, the URL also contains the product name, the name of the product line, and a specific feature for which users may be looking. While optimizing URL's, you want to strike a balance between including the right target keywords and avoiding an excessively long URL.

Image Alt Text

Alt text is technically used for accessibility purposes, as screen readers will read alt text for visually impaired readers. From an SEO perspective, alt tags provide search engines with more details on the context of an image. To optimize image alt text, focus on naturally using one of your target keywords, and be descriptive. For example:

"Nikon D500 DX 4K DSLR Camera"

Screaming Frog is great at identifying missing alt tags in bulk, but also SEOptimer's Image Alt Tag Checker will find missing alt tags, and the tool is free.

30-Day Challenge:
Optimize the Top 5 Opportunity Pages on Your Website

Go re-read the section in this chapter about prioritizing your SEO efforts. I want you to identify your *top 5* page opportunities. That's it, five pages. They should have high search volume or existing traffic and be primed to rank better and drive more traffic once optimized.

Follow the step-by-step process I've outlined to optimize each of these five pages thoroughly. Then I want you to set a reminder to check in on these pages at least once a month for the next six months. If you've done well, you'll see traffic increasing to these pages!

Off-Page SEO

While I prefer technical SEO and on-page SEO tactics because they're focused on an "owned" asset (your website), off-page SEO can be a viable traffic-generation tactic when done right.

I often prioritize off-page SEO last when developing an SEO strategy because it can be time-consuming and doesn't always yield results. On the other hand, for smaller sites, there's only so much SEO that you can do before you're simply re-optimizing your previous optimizations. Let's dig into some of the off-page SEO tactics that you can take advantage of to drive more traffic to your site.

Link Building

Let's start with the good part - quality inbound links are one of the strongest ranking signals that Google uses. It makes sense. If several high-quality, reputable websites link to a certain page on your site, it's likely a valuable page.

The best links come from reputable sites; herein lies the challenge - acquiring links from high-quality, reputable sites is tough. It's not impossible, but it can be time-consuming and in some cases lead to a dead end.

Here are some ways to approach link building in a time-effective manner:

1. **Start with "low-hanging fruit"** - Build a list of your partners, customers, suppliers, vendors, associations, affiliations, and any other organization with which you have already developed a relationship. Reach out to the organizations that make sense with a compelling reason for them to link back to your website.

For example, for associations that you're a member of, they'll often provide a directory of all of their members.

2. **Guest blogging** - Research the most trusted blogs and online publications in your industry. Identify the types of content that they already publish, and reach out to them with a compelling idea for guest content that you can write for their site. Make sure you customize this outreach and get a firm commitment from them before actually producing the content.

3. **Identify valuable directories.** Directories are a very slippery slope. There are a lot of directories out there that are very low-quality and offer very limited upside in terms of search signals. For spammy directories, you may even be penalized by search engines. Typically, the best ones are industry-specific directories and listings.

4. **Unlinked mentions.** Still staying on the trend of lower effort tactics, finding places that your company or website is mentioned online without a link is a great tactic to use. Do some research on your brand name, find mentions, and reach out to the websites that haven't included a link back to your site. SEMRush has a great brand monitoring tool to make this automatic and continuous. You'll commonly find these opportunities in online newspapers or journals and industry sites.

5. **Research competitor backlinks.** If you want to get a little more sophisticated, you can begin researching where your competitors have backlinks from and target those websites for additional link building opportunities. Most SEO platforms, my favorite being SEMRush, allow you to do this research quickly and easily.

There are certainly more link building tactics, but beyond the ones I've mentioned above, they begin to get time-consuming and complex.

Social Media

There's a reason we have a whole chapter dedicated to Social Media in this book - it can be an incredibly useful tool for increasing website traffic. To avoid being redundant with the deep dive you'll get later in that chapter, I'll point out a few points as it relates to off-page SEO:

- **Wildfire.** Links to your site from social media *may* be a ranking signal, but they're typically not very strong. Where I've seen social media *really* impact SEO is when a piece of content goes viral - it spreads like wildfire. Now, I never recommend writing a piece of content with the intent of having it go viral, but the more compelling you can make your content through unique ideas and visuals, the higher the likelihood that your content will receive higher engagement on social media.

- **Social media as a search result.** While a social media link or two won't propel your site into the top of the rankings, posts from social media *can* show up in search results themselves. You'll often see this with very topical or timely content, for example, a national/worldwide event or natural disaster. Posting regularly creates another avenue for your content to show up in search results.

Online PR

One final tactic to improve your off-page SEO is online PR. In essence, you're trying to create and distribute noteworthy or interesting news about you or your company in a free or cost-effective way. Here are some tips:

- **Make it interesting.** I hate to break it to you, but nobody cares that your company just celebrated its 10th anniversary. Journalists and online publications *do* care about press releases whose subject matter is innovative, topical, local, or just generally interesting. Innovative product launches, expansion into new local markets, or stories tied to a current event are much more likely to get "picked up."
- **Target your outreach.** If you're going after free publication of your press release, it's generally not a good idea to start by sending it to Forbes and hoping they respond. Identify the right niche publications and sites to reach out to and personalize your outreach.
- **When in doubt, pay for distribution.** There are several trustworthy press release distribution services out there that, for a fee, will get your content published across the web. Cision, formerly known as PRWeb, is probably the most well-known.

Summary

At this point, you should have a well-established content strategy and a plan of attack for SEO. Remember, content and SEO will be hugely valuable for your long-term site growth, but keep in mind that it won't happen overnight. I urge you to be patient.

I can't tell you how many times I've seen individuals or organizations give up after month one or two when they don't see immediate results. Trust me, I'm impatient. We all want to see immediate results. But outlining the right strategy, mixed with a little faith that you will gain traction, and you'll start seeing the results you want.

Your SEO Toolbox

- **SEMRush** - My vote for the best all-around SEO platform for the money. I use it for everything from finding SEO opportunities, performing keyword research, leveraging their Writing Assistant in Google Docs for writing better content, and more. *(Starts at $99/month)*
- **Google Search Console** – An excellent, free tool that allows you to view real search data from Google including impressions, clicks, and clickthrough rates. Also allows you to view technical issues or mobile usability issues.
- **Google PageSpeed Insights** - PageSpeed Insights analyzes the content of a web page, then generates suggestions to make that page faster.
- **Answer the Public** - The best tool for identifying questions that users ask related to a specific keyword. I use this every time I perform research for optimizing a page. *(Free with limitations; Pro version - $99/year)*

- **KeySearch** - My pick for the best low-cost alternative to more expensive SEO suites. A great tool for keyword research and topic research.
- **WordTracker** - Another cost-effective alternative to more expensive SEO suites, focused on SEO and PPC research. *(Starts at $27/month)*
- **SpyFu** – An SEO tool pretty specifically focused on paid and organic research; great for competitor research. *(Starts at $39/month)*
- **KeywordTool.io** – A great tool for getting autocomplete suggestions from search engines in bulk, perfect for keyword ideas. *(Free version is probably enough for most users; Pro starts at $89/month)*
- **Infinite Suggest** - Another great (and free) tool for autocomplete suggestions from search engines.
- **LSIGraph** – This is my absolute favorite tool to generate LSI (latent semantic index) keywords. Think "related" keywords. *(3 free searches per day; Paid version starts at $27/month and is worth the money)*
- **Ubersuggest** – A free tool for researching keyword and content ideas, top website pages by backlinks and social shares, and performing a basic site audit.

Digital Advertising (PPC)

Let's preface this entire chapter by saying, sure, you could *pay* your way to doubling your traffic. For many established businesses or even startups with established investment capital, this is a viable strategy.

For the sake of this book, I'm going to assume you don't have a big well of advertising funds from which to pull. We'll start from a shoestring budget, and for those who have larger marketing budgets, you can scale up using the same principles.

Establishing a Budget

How much *should* you budget for digital advertising every month? The answer, of course, is it depends on several factors:

1. **Marketing budget available** - Before you start, establish a monthly marketing budget with which you're comfortable. For some, this may start at $100 per month; for others, it may be thousands of dollars per month and up.

2. **Number of advertising networks** - In this chapter, we'll look into how to evaluate different advertising networks to identify the ones that suit your audience best.

3. **Cost of advertising in your industry** - Every industry and audience will have different advertising costs. For example, legal and insurance services notoriously have some of the most expensive advertising costs due to higher competition.

Choosing Digital Advertising Networks

Before we get too far, it's best to gain a solid understanding of the advertising networks that are available and the factors in choosing them. The major factors that go into choosing digital advertising networks include audience, ad delivery types, and costs.

The two digital advertising networks that I highly recommend starting with are Facebook Ads and Google Ads. For newcomers to digital advertising, or even those who have experimented with digital advertising in the past, these two platforms dominate the digital advertising space and should help you drive traffic no matter your budget or your audience.

Bonus Tool:
Quantcast Measure

A critical precursor to choosing the right digital advertising networks is understanding your audience. One of my favorite tools to gain a deeper understanding of a website's audience is Quantcast Measure, which, as of this writing, is a free tool.

Within a few days after simple installation, you'll be able to see valuable demographic and psychographic data on your users that will help you make an informed decision about which ad networks and audiences make sense for you.

Facebook Ads

I'm listing Facebook Ads first because when it comes to doubling your website traffic, this is typically going to be the most efficient and cost-effective channel for achieving this goal. As of July 2019, Facebook had 2.41 billion monthly active users, 1.59 billion of which log in *every day*. Simply put, this is a huge, engaged audience.

One of the other unique features of the Facebook Ads platform is the ability to also advertise on Instagram, which has 1+ billion users of its own.

Audience

Facebook was, at one time the social network of choice for college students and twentysomethings. However, today, there is a much more broad distribution across age groups.

The 25-34 demographic continues to have the most users (around 12% of all users), though it is followed closely by the 35-44 demographic (around 9%) and 45-54 demographic (around 8%). Facebook also has plenty of users in the 18-24, 55-64, and 65+ age groups, but very few below the age of 18.

Across the board, Facebook skews slightly more female in terms of users. Around 53% of users are female as of 2019.

Instagram, as you may have guessed, skews much more toward a younger demographic. The network's major age groups are 18-24 (32% of users) and 25-34 (33% of users). The platform has fewer users over the age of 45.

The gender split on Instagram is nearly even, with 50.3% of users being female.

One of the best features of Facebook Ads is the extensive Audiences that you're able to create within the platform, including remarketing audiences to target users that have already visited your website, and lookalike audiences that allow you to target users similar to your existing customers.

Ad Delivery Types

Another benefit of advertising on Facebook is the platform has a huge variety of ad types, including images, videos, interactive ads, shopping ads, and more. Most ad delivery types are available on both Facebook and Instagram platforms.

- **Photo** - The most common Facebook ad format with an image, text, and a call-to-action.
- **Video** - Plenty of options, including video ads that show in a feed, during existing video streams, and more.
- **Messenger** - Start conversations with prospects directly in Facebook Messenger.
- **Stories** - Edge-to-edge experience that lets you build immersive ad content.

Costs

Generally speaking, Facebook/Instagram is going to be the most cost-effective ad network of the *major* networks, excluding pure display advertising (think banner ads). Facebook/Instagram costs are going to depend on which "campaign objective" you choose. Some examples of these campaign objectives are:

- Traffic (the objective we'll focus on in this book)
- Engagement
- Lead generation
- Conversions

I have found success in each of these campaign objectives offered by Facebook, so don't hesitate to try one out if your goals are different.

When you focus your campaign objective on traffic, the cost model (bidding type) is cost-per-click, also known as CPC. You can expect CPC on Facebook and Instagram to be **between $.50 and $2.00**, of course, varying by industry and audience size.

Facebook Ads Strategy

If you've identified that Facebook is the right fit for your budget and the audience you're targeting, it's time to put together a strategy. There are two critical elements of a Facebook Ads strategy: **audience** and **content**.

When you're starting to build out your Facebook campaign, the first step is to choose **Traffic** as your campaign objective. Choosing your campaign objective will allow you to maximize traffic to your website.

Audience

If you're just getting started, I highly recommend starting with a **lookalike audience**, especially if you have a decent-size customer list (needs to be 1,000+ email addresses). Facebook's algorithms typically do an excellent job of finding users similar to your existing customers.

If you *don't* have a quality email list with enough contacts, then you can still use **Detailed Targeting** effectively. You can target users based on data points like interests, job titles, fields of study, employers, and more. Hopefully you know your audience better than anyone else, and you can use Detailed Targeting to start with the right mix of demographics, interests, and behaviors.

Be cautious with **age and gender targeting**, as you may inadvertently disclude users that may be interested in your products, services or content. I typically recommend leaving these more open at first, then looking at Facebook's analytics after a few weeks to see if you need to narrow this down at all.

Don't forget to leverage **geographic targeting**, especially if your business or organization is local or regional. If you serve people nationally, then one way to work with a smaller budget is to choose a targeted geographic location to pilot your campaign before you go national.

You'll see the option to choose "when you get charged" by Facebook - by impression or by link click. Since we're focused on driving traffic, I would recommend selecting **"link click (CPC)"** to start. If you feel that you can craft ads that have exceptionally high clickthrough rates, then you may want to consider paying for impressions, but this probably isn't the best route for those just starting out.

You'll also see an option for delivery type. Unless the content of your advertisement is time-sensitive, for example, an upcoming event or product launch, I would recommend **"Standard"** delivery, which will deliver ads evenly throughout your selected schedule.

Content (Ads)

The next step is to think about *what* to put in front of your audience. Hopefully, when you built your audience, you already had this in the back of your mind. This may be an obvious statement, but you need to really think about what this audience wants and needs.

Here's an easy way to fail: pick an audience that you *want* to visit your website and show them content that you *think* they may like. You need to have a deep understanding of what is compelling to this audience.

Remember, you can use a tool like Quantcast Measure to get a better understanding of your users' demographics and behavior.

With Facebook ads, you have a few different components:

- Headline
- Image
- Main text
- News feed link description
- Call-to-action

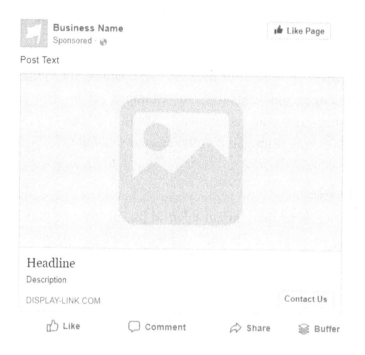

Let's get into how to put together the perfect Facebook ad. Here are the steps:

1. **Keep your headline concise and catchy.** Try to focus on around five words for your headline to ensure that it doesn't get cut off. Focus on actionable words like "See," "Get," or "Read." For example, if you want users to read your latest

piece of content on the Keto Diet, try out "Read our Keto Diet Guide." Short, simple and actionable.

2. **Focus on around 20 words of main ad text.** This is where you *really* need to understand your audience. Use any keyword research you've done up until this point and use the language your audience uses. Some additional tactics for more compelling ad text include using numbered lists, creating a sense of urgency for your offer, and being *very* clear about what the user will be getting (or seeing) after they click.

3. **Write a link description under 30 characters.** Again, with such a limited character count, you need to be concise, actionable, and to the point. Using our Keto Diet Guide example, you may use something like, "Feel better than ever," and play up to the emotional and physical feelings of users.

4. **Use the right call-to-action.** First of all, make sure the call-to-action language you're using is appropriate for the content. According to research from AdEspresso, the top calls-to-action in terms of clickthrough rate are:
   a. Learn More
   b. *None*
   c. Shop Now
   d. Sign Up
   e. Book Travel

5. **Use eye-catching images.** I'm telling you now, if you use a drab stock image of a diverse group of business professionals sitting at a meeting table, your ad will suck. People will scroll right past. You need a picture that will slow the pace of a user's quick scrolling and capture their attention. Here are some themes that are proven to work:
   a. People using *your* product(s)

71

b. People that match *your* target audience
c. Complementary or contrasting colors
d. Bright colors
e. High-resolution, unique images

Now that you've crafted a well thought-out ad, here's the next important step: create two more. I don't care if you believe you've perfected this ad; it's always a good idea to test at least 2-3 ads at a time to identify which one will perform better. Test slightly different text, a different image, and a different call-to-action if another option works.

After a short amount of time, the results will speak for themselves. You're looking for the ad or ads that have the highest clickthrough rates at the lowest cost-per-click.

Once you feel confident that you've identified a top-performing ad, build two more based on that and pause the others. Consider using the same image, but slightly modifying the ad text. Or, vice versa, consider using the same ad text but using a slightly different image.

Google Ads

Google's advertising network provides robust advertising options for both search advertising and display advertising. On the search advertising side, if you focus your keyword research on longtail keywords, they can be quite affordable. Remember, longtail keywords are more specific, detailed, and descriptive.

While display advertising is generally a very cost-effective medium for getting *impressions*, I am generally less bullish on the medium for high-quality traffic and conversions. You'll find *plenty* of experts that will disagree, and I won't dissuade you from trying it as part of your strategy. However, in this book, we're going to be focusing on search advertising.

Audience

The great thing about Google is essentially *everyone* uses it, as it's by far the most-used search engine. With Google Ads, your "audience" targeting is going to focus on keywords and intent more so than demographics. In this case, you're targeting those who are looking for specific keywords, topics, or content.

Just as with Facebook, you'll be able to set up remarketing audiences to users that have already visited your site - or even specific pages on your site. As of late, Google has begun to offer a few different additional types of audience targeting:

- **In-Market audiences** - Customers that are actively researching or buying within a specific market.
- **Customer Match** - Target existing customers/prospects or identify audiences similar to those users.

Ad Delivery Types

Whereas Facebook is a more dynamic network that allows a wide variety of ad types, Google Ads will be more focused on text-based ads for its search network. There are a few unique varieties of text ads that Google offers, including *responsive search ads*.

Responsive search ads effectively allow you to add multiple headlines and descriptions to one ad, and Google will test different combinations to learn which combinations work best. Responsive search ads are a huge time-saver and a great use of machine learning that is available to everyone.

Ad Extensions

One of the often-overlooked features that Google Ads offers is ad extensions. These additional pieces of content allow you to get more real estate in the search results page without paying more. They also allow you to offer up additional types of information outside of your headline and description. Here are some of the ad extensions I'd encourage you to look into:

- **Location Extensions.** Displaying your location, especially for local businesses like restaurants, yoga studios, or auto mechanics, can build interest for local searchers. It can also build trust for searchers that are looking for a local resource as opposed to a big, nationwide chain or company.
- **Call Extensions.** Ok, to be fair, this isn't going to increase your site traffic. I'll call myself out on that. But it's too important to ignore. Call extensions allow you to add your phone number to your ad, giving users the ability to call directly from the search results page.
- **Sitelink Extensions.** These allow you to add additional site pages to your ad that may be relevant. Think of related products or services, contact pages, testimonials, and "about" pages.
- **Structured Snippet Extensions.** These extensions allow you to list specific products, services, or other listable information. For example, if you run a yoga studio, you could list the types of classes that you offer, such as "hot yoga," "prenatal yoga," or "beginner's yoga."

- **Price Extensions.** If you offer products or services that have defined prices, the price extension is a great way to both set user expectations, and filter out users that don't fit within your price range. For example, an auto mechanic could put the price of an oil change directly in their ad.

Costs

There are several different bid strategies that Google Ads offers. There are bid strategies catered to maximizing conversions, awareness, interactions, and most importantly in our case, traffic. I believe each of these bid strategies is viable depending on your goals, but since we're focused on increasing traffic - we're going to focus on the *Maximize Clicks* bid strategy.

Maximize Clicks allows even novice Google Ads users to focus on traffic by setting a daily budget and letting Google automate bidding to maximize the number of clicks, and as a result, traffic to your site.

Google Ads Strategy

There are many differences between Google Ads and Facebook Ads, but the one *key* differentiator to keep top of mind is search intent. On Facebook, you're targeting an audience based on demographics and behavior, whereas on Google Ads, you're targeting an audience based on search intent.

You don't *necessarily* know who your Google Ads audience is, although there are increasingly better ways to target demographics or behavior. Instead, you're focusing on *what* a user is looking for. Therefore the two critical elements that we're going to dive into are **keywords** and **content (ads)**.

Keywords

On Google Ads, keywords are your primary targeting mechanism. To find the best keywords, you need to think like your audience. What are the keywords that they're typing into search engines to find the content, products, services, and information that your site has to offer? Here's how to find out by doing **keyword research** in a spreadsheet:

1. **Qualitative Research.** Start by putting yourself in the mindset of your audience. What are the keywords they're searching for? Document a few of these. If your creativity is flowing, go for 50-100 keywords. If you're unsure, try for ten ideas.

2. **Research Tools.** There is an almost limitless amount of tools that allow you to research keywords for your Google Ads campaigns. Some are free that are powerful but have limitations, and then there are more robust tools that carry a monthly cost.

3. **Competitor Research.** One of the best ways to get keyword ideas is to see what your top competitors are bidding on. This is the real value of paid keyword research tools, as any of the three listed on the next page will give you detailed intel and recommendations on what keywords your competitors are bidding on and with which they're having success.

Digital Advertising Keyword Research Tools

Free Keyword Research Tools	Paid Keyword Research Tools
Google Ads Keyword Planner - Free tool offered by Google for advertisers that gives recommendations, search volume, and average cost-per-click (CPC).	**SEMRush** - Robust Google Ads keyword research tool that provides you with volume, keyword difficulty, and average CPC.
Infinite Suggest - Allows you to put in a seed keyword and see hundreds of Google autocomplete suggestions.	**SpyFu** - Their Adwords Advisor gives keyword recommendations based on your competitors' success and gives simple "buy" ratings to guide you.
Keywordtool.io - Another great Google autocomplete suggestion tool. (Has a paid option)	**Keysearch** - Multiple keyword suggestion options including search volume, CPC & PPC.

Once you have a list of keywords put together in a spreadsheet, it's important to understand keyword search volume, cost, and competition. Simply set up your spreadsheet like this:

Keyword	Search Volume (Monthly)	CPC	Competition

If you're looking for a free way to do this, you can paste your keywords into Google Keyword Planner and it will give you an estimated monthly search volume, CPC range, and a sense of competition (Low, Medium, High). The data is *pretty* good for a free tool, and it's coming right from Google, so it has a high degree of validity. There are some shortcomings with the data that Google's Keyword Planner provides:

- Search volume ranges are often wide, so it's hard to get a good sense of real search volume, and there's not a historical trend to show seasonality or history.
- Competition is only represented as "Low," "Medium," or "High." I'd rather rely on tools that provide me a more specific numeric competition value.
- Average CPC is now separated by "high range" and "low range" for the "Top of page" position only, which can be confusing and limiting.

When I'm looking for detailed data to add to my keyword research spreadsheet, I'm typically relying on better platforms like SEMRush or SpyFu.

Once you have your spreadsheet complete with all of your keywords, search volume, costs, and competition, it's time to organize them. Start by grouping similar keywords into **Ad Groups**. These are groups of keywords that are similar based on your products, services or other categories. Grouping keywords will allow you to create tailored ads for each ad group of similar keywords later on.

The final thing you need to consider when doing your keyword research is if you will let Google modify your keywords by using different keyword match types. Here are the options and how Google defines them:

- **Phrase Match** - Matches the phrase (or close variations of the phrase) with additional words before or after. For example, if the keyword is "yoga studio," your ad could also show for the search term "hot yoga studio."
- **Exact Match** - Exact matches of the term. With this match type, no additional words before or after will be considered.
- **Broad Match** - Matches close variations of the keyword, related searches, and other relevant variations. The words in the keyword don't have to be present in a user's search.

Here's a quick reference guide for how to input these keywords into Google Ads using special symbols to indicate each different match type:

Keyword Match Type	Symbol	Example
Phrase Match	"baseball cards"	Baseball cards Topps baseball cards Baseball cards
Exact Match	[baseball cards]	Baseball cards
Broad Match	baseball cards	Baseball cards Basketball cards Baseball collectibles

There are several different schools of thought regarding which keyword match types to use. I want to present two simple strategies that you can choose from to begin:

Strategy #1: Broad Match with Negative Keywords

Using this strategy, you'll launch your Google Ads campaign with broad match keywords. This means that you'll be allowing Google to bid on "related" keywords to show your ads. The benefit of this strategy is that you'll have the widest reach initially. The risk of this strategy is that you're allowing Google to bid on keywords that you haven't explicitly chosen, meaning some or many of them may be irrelevant to your audience or your business.

The best way to combat this issue of bidding on low-quality keywords is to implement **negative keywords**. Identifying a negative keyword prevents your ad from being triggered by a certain word or phrase. You can start by adding a few negative keywords to your campaign or ad group before you launch, but it's most important to constantly monitor the search terms that are triggering your ads and add low-quality keywords to your negative keywords list.

Strategy #2: Exact Match or Phrase Match

This strategy is essentially the opposite of Strategy #1. Instead of casting a wide net, you're only showing your ads for the exact keywords or phrases that you've identified. The benefit of this strategy is that you'll limit the amount of low-quality keywords that are triggering your ads. The risk with this strategy is that if you have too few keywords or low-volume keywords, you may not see the overall volume to drive the traffic you need.

If you do implement this strategy, monitor your daily exposure and ad spend. If you're not reaching your daily budget, you'll want to consider either adding additional keywords or expanding some of your keywords to phrase match or broad match over time.

Content (Ads)

Google Ads are going to be different than Facebook ads in that the ad types we're focusing on are purely text-based search ads. You won't be able to leverage any images, so you're going to need to write compelling and focused ad copy.

Hopefully by now, you've grouped your keywords into relevant Ad Groups by product, service, or some other theme. By doing this, your ads should theoretically be applicable and relevant to any of the keywords you've included in each keyword group.

Start with Responsive Search Ads

If you haven't run Google Ads before, I highly recommend starting with Google's newer responsive search ads (still in beta as of the publishing of this book). Responsive search ads allow you to add multiple headlines and descriptions to one ad, and over time, Google

Ads will automatically test different combinations to learn which combinations perform best. Responsive Search Ads are an excellent way to save time on individually creating multiple ads. It also lets you take advantage of machine learning to let higher-performing ads rise to the top.

Tips for Writing High-Performing Search Ads

1. **Match the User's Search Intent.** When writing your ad, put yourself in the shoes of the user and predict *exactly* what they're looking for. If the user is searching for "wedding photographer," don't get too crazy in your ad talking about newborn photography or family portraits. The user is clearly looking for one *specific* thing, and you need to convince them that your result meets their needs.

2. **Use Keywords.** Try your best to mirror the user's query (the keywords on which you're bidding) in your ad copy. If a user is searching for "get rid of acne," rather than showing a generic "Dermatologist - Philadelphia, PA" ad, mimic their search term for better results: "Talk to a doctor about getting rid of your acne once and for all."

3. **Be Specific.** Generic ads get lost in the crowd. Simply saying "the best restaurant around" ends up not saying a whole lot. Instead, list specifics: "Named the best Italian restaurant by Culinary Magazine."

4. **Include a Call-to-Action.** Don't leave your users guessing what the next step is. Include a call-to-action like "Schedule an appointment," "Learn more," "Buy Now," or another relevant, actionable phrase.

Landing Pages

Once you've identified the perfect keywords for your ad campaign, organized them in related Ad Groups, and written bulletproof ad copy for each Ad Group, it's important to consider the landing page. After all, you've spent all of this time researching keywords and writing ad copy; you don't want to lose your audience when they get to your site.

While we won't get too deep into building killer landing pages from scratch, I do want to introduce a few recommendations to ensure your Google Ads perform well:

- **Focus on relevance.** In an ideal world, you're building a completely customized landing page catered to every ad group. The copy on these landing pages should be focused on the keywords, user intent, and should carry through the language you've used in your ads.
- **Find the best fit.** When you can't create brand new landing pages for each ad group in your Google Ads campaign, ensure that you're linking each ad to the most *relevant* page that exists on your site today.

If you don't have the flexibility to edit your site or create well-designed pages from scratch, one of my favorite landing page builders is **Unbounce**, which lets you use pre-built templates and a drag-and-drop editor to build awesome PPC landing pages.

30-Day Challenge:
Produce a High-Performing Ad

Whether you've decided to advertise on Facebook, Google, or possibly one of the other ad networks we'll discuss in the next section, having just *one* ad that performs really well can give you enough traction and motivation upon which to build.

If you're using Facebook, focus on building several ad variations with different images and ad copy. In Google Ads, try out responsive ads to let Google test different variations for you. Go through *at least* three iterations to keep building upon successful ads to get to a point where you have a high-performing ad that's driving lots of traffic at an affordable cost-per-click (CPC).

Other Ad Networks

While I've detailed two of the tried-and-true networks for driving quality traffic to your site, there are many other ad platforms and networks to consider. Rather than diving deep into any single one, I wanted to list some of the top networks and a brief overview of their place in the market.

- **LinkedIn Ads** - This is a terrific platform for B2B organizations targeting business professionals. I've found it to be significantly better at generating *leads* than cost-effectively driving website traffic.
- **Bing Ads** - Quite similar to Google Ads, though with a smaller user base. There are some nice integrations with LinkedIn data (LinkedIn is owned by Microsoft), but I wouldn't look into Bing until I was comfortable with Google Ads.
- **Pinterest Ads** - If you're familiar with Pinterest, then you know this social network skews significantly more female and the content tends to be focused on arts and crafts, food and drink, home and garden, health and beauty, and clothing and apparel.
- **Display Advertising / Programmatic** - As I mentioned previously, I'm not a huge believer in display advertising in the absence of a bigger, more integrated strategy. It *does* have the potential to drive cost-effective traffic if done right, and can also be effective in building a remarketing list for search or social.

Summary

In most cases, especially if you're a novice to digital advertising, I'd recommend you start with Facebook Ads or Google Ads. The networks are large, they're affordable, they both use machine learning to optimize your campaigns for you (if you choose), and you can find plenty of support and recommendations for both platforms.

Remember, the focus of paid digital advertising isn't to pay your way to doubling your traffic. It's to use the medium as one of the tools in your toolkit to target highly-relevant users and get them to your site in a cost-effective manner.

Your Digital Advertising Toolbox

- **SpyFu** - My top tool for PPC competitor research, in addition to keyword research and suggestions. *(Starts at $39/month)*
- **SEMRush** - Great for paid keyword research, competitor research, assistance with writing ad copy, and monitoring digital advertising performance. *(Try it for free using the link above; Starts at $99/month)*
- **Google Ads Keyword Planner** - One of the essential tools for performing keyword research when running Google Ads.
- **Infinite Suggest** - Allows you to put in a seed keyword and see hundreds of Google autocomplete suggestions.
- **Keywordtool.io** - Another great Google autocomplete suggestion tool. *(Has a paid option)*
- **Keysearch** - Multiple keyword suggestion options including search volume, CPC, and PPC.

- **Quantcast Measure** - A useful free tool for gaining a better understanding of your audience before diving into digital advertising.

Social Media

The final chapter in this book is focused on social media, and how we can leverage this medium to drive traffic to your site. The entire notion of this chapter is ironically a bit counterintuitive to the concept of social media, which is meant to be a medium through which users can engage *on* the platforms themselves.

Let's establish that in-network engagement is a really important element of social media for marketing. For the sake of this chapter, we're going to be focused on driving traffic *from* these social networks.

Choosing the Right Social Networks

Just as with digital advertising, it's really important to choose the *right* social networks that match two things:

1. Where your audience is
2. The type of content you want to share

For example, if you're targeting 35-45-year-old mothers, you may look to Facebook and Pinterest. If your content is very visual, you'll consider Instagram and Pinterest. If you want to share thought leadership content, you could look to Twitter or LinkedIn.

If you already have a social media presence, I would highly encourage you to re-evaluate the channels on which you're active, and where you plan to focus. You'll see better results if you focus on 2-3 highly relevant social media channels than if you try to spread yourself too thin on too many social networks.

Here are some tips for pinpointing the social networks that are right for you:

1. **Match Platform and Audience** - As mentioned above, you'll want to consider where your audience typically "hangs out" digitally. Blogger Angie Gensler has an excellent infographic that matches audiences with each social network:

   https://www.angiegensler.com/how-to-choose-the-right-social-media-platform-for-your-business/

2. **Research Your Competitors** - Identify your top 2-3 competitors and research their social media presence. Just *having* a presence on a particular social media platform isn't necessarily a good indication that it's working. You're looking for channels through which they have a lot of followers and strong engagement.

3. **Consider Your Goals** - If we're sticking with the assumption that your primary goal is driving traffic back to your site, certain platforms may be a better fit than others. For example, Instagram doesn't offer up a lot of opportunities to include links back to your site and is more focused on in-platform engagement.

Building Your Social Media Audience

You've heard the old adage, "If a tree falls in the woods and no one is there to hear it..." Well, the same goes for social media - you don't want to be shouting your message with no one there to hear it.

If you have an already-established social media presence, it's a good time to take inventory of your audience on each social network. This is, of course, quite relative. Major companies, brands, and influencers are naturally going to have audiences in the millions and beyond.

Here are several tips for ensuring you have a solid audience foundation before ramping up your social media efforts:

1. **Follow, Connect, Join** - Depending on the network, focus on following and connecting with relevant users and joining relevant communities. In many cases, these users will follow you back, as will those participating in the same communities as you.

2. **Use Hashtags** - As you continue to post, leverage relevant hashtags in each network to ensure that your content is findable and those interested in that topic can follow your content.

3. **Add Social Media Links** - Allow your audience and customers to follow you on social media through social media links. Consider adding them to your website, email signature, and marketing emails you send out. Even better, set expectations for what potential followers can expect in terms of content and frequency.

Using Social Media to Drive Website Traffic

You have your two-to-three targeted social networks picked out, you've been actively working on building your audience, and now it's time to throw some gas on the social media fire.

Posting More - A *Lot* More

I want you to think about how you and others around you use social media. If you're like most people, you access one or more social networks multiple times a day and scroll through your feed until you find something interesting. You may spend a few seconds dwelling before continuing, and if something *really* catches your eye, you may take the time to read it, watch it, or follow a link to learn more.

When scrolling like this, users see probably less than an hour's worth of content. Here is why I bring this up: many businesses and marketers limit their posts to at most one per day for fear of overwhelming their audience. The reality, though, is that by doing this, they are likely risking their audience not seeing their content at all that day (or week, or month).

The remedy: post more. A lot more. Here's how to approach this:

1. **Test posting frequency tolerance** - Ideally, you want to identify the maximum number of posts that you can share each day without overwhelming followers to the point of unfollowing. Now isn't the time or place to be conservative. If you've been posting three times per week, deciding to post once every day isn't enough. Try posting *five* times per day and see how your audience reacts.

2. **Post similar content multiple times** - Brands and entrepreneurs are often timid about posting similar content in a

short period of time. The reality is the likelihood of a follower seeing that content multiple times is relatively low. Alternately, there's some science behind people seeing content two or three times before they actually engage with it. You want to avoid posting the *exact* same content within a short period of time, so make sure you tweak the language for each post.

3. **Leverage social posting software.** I'm sure you're reading this thinking, "Five posts per *day??* How will I have the time to do this?" Certainly not by logging into each social network five times per day to post. You need to leverage social posting software to scale your content posting efforts. In the next section, I'll detail some of my favorite social media tools.

Bonus Tool:
Canva

If you're going to be posting a *lot* more content, you're going to need some additional resources to do so. Canva is a great platform for users with little-to-no design chops to create quality images, infographics, quotes, and more that can be used on social media.

Social Media Posting Platforms

Now that we've established the goal of increasing social media posting frequency, we need a plan for how to do this at scale. This is where social media posting platforms come in. Sure you could go to each social network you're using five times a day and post, but who has the time for that? Here are some of the specific tools that I would recommend to automate this process:

- **Buffer** – An incredibly easy user interface that allows you to add content into a "bucket" and Buffer will share it on a schedule you choose. It also has a handy Google Chrome plugin that allows you to add content to your schedule right from any page on the web. Buffer connects with all of the major social platforms and provides great analytics. Their free version will be enough to try it out, but you'll likely want to upgrade to at least the next tier to really automate your social media workflow.

- **Hootsuite** - Similar to Buffer, although I find Buffer's interface to be slightly easier to use. Hootsuite has some additional features that Buffer doesn't have, like content curation and discovery, but their main feature set is quite similar. Hootsuite offers a free tier to get you started and then, much like Buffer, you can upgrade as you scale up.

- **SocialOomph** - A simpler platform without some of the bells-and-whistles of the platforms above, but the price point is more affordable. They offer a free version, and upgrading costs as little as $15/month. They pride themselves on doing one thing very well with high customer satisfaction rates.

- **Sendible** – This is a more robust social media management platform that offers social posting automation, but also monitoring, content curation, and more advanced analytics. It works well for those managing social media accounts for multiple brands or websites.

- **SproutSocial** - Probably the most costly out of this group, but justified by their position as an industry leader in this space. A better fit for brands, agencies, and enterprise clients, the full-featured platform starts at $99/month.

30-Day Challenge:
10X Your Social Media Content Production

This isn't the book that's going to recommend you post three times per week. I want to push your posting threshold until you see signs of fatigue. That means for 30 days I want you to post *ten times* more content than you currently do.

If you're not using social media at all, I want you to methodically pick *one* platform and post ten times per week on it. If you're currently using social media and posting three times per week, I want you to post 30 times per week. Space those posts out and don't be afraid to post on the weekends. Use a tool to help you batch all of this content and schedule it. Do this for one month and assess your results.

Getting More Out of Each Piece of Content

Some of the aforementioned social media publishing platforms allow you to set up a social media content calendar, similar to the content calendar we put together in the first chapter. A social media content calendar is helpful to visualize when you're posting your content, but in the absence of a formal calendar, you can also establish some posting guidelines for new content that will help you systematize social media publishing. Here's an example:

After you publish a new piece of content on your website, schedule several posts based on a set cadence:

- **Immediate** - Share a message immediately after the new content is published.
- **That Day** - The same day, share a few additional snippets from your new piece of content, whether they be quotes, images, statistics, or other short blurbs.
- **Next Day** - Keep your new content fresh by sharing a "just published" message.
- **Next Week** - Schedule a couple more short snippets, or even better, tag other users or sources that you've referenced in your content.
- **Next Month** - Schedule a few "in case you missed it" posts to keep your content in front of your audience.
- **Ongoing** - Share at least one post every month for the next couple of months. Put a spin on your posts by asking your audience a question or calling out a different aspect of your content.

As a reminder, you'll want to avoid sharing the *exact* same message multiple times. Social media platforms have been cracking down on this, and their algorithms don't like duplicate content just as much as Google doesn't like duplicate content. Remember to keep each social media post unique and varied.

Posting at the Right Times

I'm not a huge advocate of getting too focused on timing every social media post perfectly. I believe that the more you post, you'll get a better sense of the days and times that work well for you. However, I also love to leverage real data when it's accessible to me. One of my favorite tools for understanding when *my* audience is the most active on social media is Followerwonk. One of the features of the free version of this tool is the ability to determine what time of day your audience is most active.

Make Your Content Easy to Share

The easier it is for your website visitors to share content directly from your site, the better the chances you have to create an army of advocates that share your content with *their* audience.

The most common form of this tactic is leveraging social media sharing buttons included directly on your content. Some site templates or designers will include this functionality automatically. For those of you that don't currently have this functionality, AddThis is probably the most popular and easiest way to add social sharing buttons to your website. Bonus - it's free!

When you're adding social sharing buttons to your site, it's important to consider context. Blog posts are commonly the type of content that users *want* to share. Product pages are also great candidates for social sharing buttons. However, I highly recommend that you think twice before slapping social sharing buttons on your "About Us" or services pages. Not to be harsh, but nobody wants to share your "About Us" page. They want to share valuable or interesting content and products that they like or want to purchase.

Become a Trusted Curator of Content

Most social media strategists will tell you that exclusively publishing your *own* content typically isn't a recipe for success. Users and followers build trust in you when you become not just a *publisher* of content, but also a *curator* of content. This means that you're trusted for finding and sharing relevant, interesting, and informative content that your target audience will love.

The benefit of becoming a curator of content is that you'll naturally have more to publish. When we talked about posting more, it's important to keep in mind that you're going to need enough unique content to publish. Here are a few ways that you can curate meaningful content:

1. **Follow industry publishers.** No matter the social platform, identify 25+ trusted industry resources, individuals, or publishers. They'll be publishing a constant stream of information that you can re-share.
2. **Use a content curation platform.** Many of the platforms mentioned above, including Hootsuite, Sendible, and SproutSocial allow you to find content based on specific topics. Other platforms to look into include Flipboard and Medium. I'd also recommend setting up Google Alerts for keywords or topics related to your area of focus.
3. **Outsource it.** You'll have to evaluate how much time social media is taking on a week-to-week basis, but platforms like Fiverr and Upwork may allow you to find a freelancer that can

curate, organize and schedule all of your content on an ongoing basis at an affordable rate.

As you share more content from third-party sources, be sure to tag them on your social network of choice, and you'll start to build relationships wherein they share your content in return!

Summary

In terms of all the tactics that we've walked through in this book, my experience is that social media can be the most challenging for brands and individuals to stick with. It's a medium focused on vanity metrics - likes, shares, comments, etc. When we receive that approval, we feel good, even if it's not driving real results like website traffic or lead generation. When we don't get that approval, we too quickly abandon the strategy.

Unless I'm working with a popular brand, individual, or organization with a well-established social media presence, I rarely rely on social media to contribute a high percentage of traffic to the websites on which I'm working. These platforms are increasingly trying to keep users *on* the social networks themselves, rather than send traffic elsewhere. Have you noticed that almost all social media platforms have rolled out ways for you to publish content directly *on* the platform?

Social media is where I encourage you to do the most testing. Test channels, test post frequency, test types of content, and test your engagement with others on social media. Find the 20% of activities that yield 80% of results (the Pareto Principle), focus on those, and be steadfast about automating social media as much as possible.

Your Social Media Toolbox

- **Buffer** – A platform to collect and automatically publish social media content on a regular schedule.
- **Hootsuite** – A social media management platform that allows you to manage all of your social media channels from one place.

- **SocialOomph** - A simpler, more cost-effective social media posting platform without many of the bells-and-whistles of some of the other platforms.
- **Sendible** – A more robust social media management platform that offers social posting automation, but also monitoring, content curation, and more advanced analytics.
- **SproutSocial** – Yet another full-featured social media management platform, commonly recognized as a leader in the industry.
- **AddThis** - An incredibly easy tool that allows you to add social sharing buttons to your website.
- **Followerwonk** – A free tool to analyze your social media followers and audience.
- **Canva** – A simple design platform for users with little to no design chops to create quality images, infographics, quotes, and more that can be used on social media.

Resources

Throughout this book, you've seen numerous examples of spreadsheets, documents, and calendars that you can use to plan, organize, and carry out your digital marketing strategy. In this section, you'll find several template pages that you can fill in or copy as you work through the exercises in this book.

Content Audit Template

URL	Pageviews	Status

Content Audit Template

URL	Pageviews	Status

Content Audit Template

URL	Pageviews	Status

Content Audit Template

URL	Pageviews	Status

Content Research Template

Topic	Target Keyword	Search Volume	Keyword Difficulty

Content Research Template

Topic	Target Keyword	Search Volume	Keyword Difficulty

Content Research Template

Topic	Target Keyword	Search Volume	Keyword Difficulty

Content Research Template

Topic	Target Keyword	Search Volume	Keyword Difficulty

Content Production Template

Page/Blog Post Title:	
Meta Title:	Meta Description:
Target Keyword:	Secondary Keywords:
LSI Keywords:	
Questions:	
Internal Links:	External Links:

Page/Blog Post Title:	
Meta Title:	Meta Description:
Target Keyword:	Secondary Keywords:
LSI Keywords:	
Questions:	
Internal Links:	External Links:

Content Production Template

Page/Blog Post Title:	
Meta Title:	Meta Description:
Target Keyword:	Secondary Keywords:
LSI Keywords:	
Questions:	
Internal Links:	External Links:

Page/Blog Post Title:	
Meta Title:	Meta Description:
Target Keyword:	Secondary Keywords:
LSI Keywords:	
Questions:	
Internal Links:	External Links:

Content Production Template

Page/Blog Post Title:	
Meta Title:	Meta Description:
Target Keyword:	Secondary Keywords:
LSI Keywords:	
Questions:	
Internal Links:	External Links:

Page/Blog Post Title:	
Meta Title:	Meta Description:
Target Keyword:	Secondary Keywords:
LSI Keywords:	
Questions:	
Internal Links:	External Links:

Content Production Template

Page/Blog Post Title:	
Meta Title:	Meta Description:
Target Keyword:	Secondary Keywords:
LSI Keywords:	
Questions:	
Internal Links:	External Links:

Page/Blog Post Title:	
Meta Title:	Meta Description:
Target Keyword:	Secondary Keywords:
LSI Keywords:	
Questions:	
Internal Links:	External Links:

Clickthrough Rate Opportunities

URL	Average CTR (Search Console)	Average Position	Average CTR (Reference)

Clickthrough Rate Opportunities

URL	Average CTR (Search Console)	Average Position	Average CTR (Reference)

Google Ads Keyword Research

Keyword	Search Volume (Monthly)	CPC	Competition

Google Ads Keyword Research

Keyword	Search Volume (Monthly)	CPC	Competition

www.ingramcontent.com/pod-product-compliance
Lightning Source LLC
Chambersburg PA
CBHW031243050326
40690CB00007B/936